Tears and Tequila

James Lightwood

Presentation by *BookLeaf Publishing*

Web: www.bookleafpub.com

E-mail: info@bookleafpub.com

ISBN: 9789357440806

First edition 2023

Genetics

20

My arms are bloody beneath my sleeves and the hospital is antiseptic
"Do you have any thoughts of harming yourself or others?"
Respectfully ma'am what the fuck do you think brought me here on a fucking Monday?
The hospital bracelet is rough plastic against my wrist with the name of somebody who doesn't exist anymore glaring up at me
"Any history of substance abuse?"
I laugh without meaning to

19
There's maybe two days a week where I'm not drunk
I tell my best friend that its okay because I work full time
I am a functional alcoholic
When I stop being functional I'll reign it in
I wake up on the floor in a puddle of vomit
I have to be at work in ten minutes and I don't know where my uniform is

I drive to work still drunk because the fun part
of blacking out
Is the bonus drunk you get in the morning
I fix my hat and apron in the mirror and I cringe
away
There's still vomit crusted on my throat
But it's okay because there's a baggie of coke in
my pocket
A little treat for working a 12 hour shift
Plus a whole jar of it at home
I may be spending every spare dime I have on
drugs
But what price can you put on feeling alive?

18
I flee family for the safety of friends
I'm sleeping on a couch in somebody's living
room and have a boss that treats me like shit
But it's okay because I smoke flower everyday
and make it my mission to drink everyone under
the table
I'm the fun kid because I never say no to shots
and I chug warm tequila straight from the bottle
at parties
I figure out very quickly how much faster you
can get drunk if your stomach is empty
Strawberry Smirnoff never tasted the same after
a man I didn't know fucked me in the back of
his jeep while I was barely conscious

I mean, he drove 45 whole minutes for a quickie
So why would he listen to "please stop" when he
was already inside me?
But it's okay because I don't feel anything but
empty
I discover my love for cocaine on a chilly Friday
night
I think it's October but I don't know and I don't
care because I haven't been sober in months
And right now
I am fucking invincable

17
My mom finds out that I'm trans
She picks me up from work and spends the
whole drive home
screaming so loudly I don't know how she can
breathe
"You fucking freak! What? Being a fucking
lesbian wasn't enough for you?"
I'm scared she might be angry enough to hit me
But she hasn't hit me since I was too small to
fight back

17
I blackout for the first time at a coworker's
birthday party
Supposedly the jungle juice is dangerous but I
don't know enough to know what that means

I laugh and sip Bacardi from someone's flask
because for once I am not
Itchy and uncomfortable and afraid of eye
contact
Three red solo cups of blue mystery shit later
and suddenly
I am outside eating chicken nuggets with a girl I
don't really know
I'm crying? She tells me it's gonna be okay
We all have shitty families

17
I am drunk at a party and somebody hands me a
dab pen
I don't know what a cross fade is but they say it's
fun
The smoke burns my lungs and I cough until I
throw up
The room is spinning but i'm dancing so maybe
that's what it is
Somehow there's a cup of something in my hand
and
Somehow I am limp in the arms of somebody
who's carrying me outside to splash water on me
and make sure I'm not dead

16

My father and I don't interact much anymore but
he hasn't hit me in three years so I can't
complain

16
My mother and I fight all the time
I can't remember a time when her anger wasn't a
livewire leaving destruction in its wake
She throws bins of clean dishes across the
kitchen and asks me why I'm such an ungrateful
little bitch
Her bedroom door slams and rattles the house on
its foundation
I can still her hear yelling about how shes going
to leave us all here
Since we all hate her anyway
She crawls into my bed that night and lays on
top of me with her head on my chest
"I'm sorry honey but you make me so angry"
They say if you encounter a bear in the wild to
play dead so it leaves you alone
And I wonder if that approach would work on
my mother

16
I try alcohol for the first time
He tells me I better finish the glass of wine
because he doesn't want it to go to waste
I don't like how it tastes

15

I tell my mother that I am a lesbian
She tells me that I am not allowed to tell
anybody else because I am just confused and
looking for attention and she doesn't want me to
make my sister confused too

13

I don't understand why I look at girls the way I
do
I don't understand why I don't feel like one
I am on tumblr trying to figure it out
Nothing about girls who feel weird but I see
something about alcoholism being genetic
It's probably good that I hate alcohol

11

Someone calls CPS on my parents for the first
time

6

I am hiding under a table listening to mama and
papa scream at each other
I don't know what they're fighting about
But I know papa used to drink too much and
hurt mama
She told me
I am never gonna drink
Because he scares me

Vices

Sometimes all I think about is you

Feeling fuzzy around the edges
Drowning in waves of warmth
Sugar sweet poison dripping down my throat

Sometimes all I think about is being invincible
White powder on my nose ring
The way your heart can beat so fast you're
practically flying
But you're just laying on the sidewalk wondering
if god feels like this too

Sometimes all I think about is how big my
pupils can get
The way the wind felt like the spirit of life
caressing my skin
The way music becomes my blood cells
The way I never want it to stop and the second it
does all I want is more
More more more
Until my bones and my brain are replaced
entirely by you

Sometimes I am all sunshine and bumble bees
and kisses that taste like cigarettes and softness
Sometimes I am thunder and violence and the
taste of shame covering my bathroom floor
Sometimes I wonder if I'll ever stop

I wish I had the answers

Knowing isn't Believing

I know the moon would continue her cycles and
the forest wouldn't mourn me
I know I am just sentient electricity
But I don't know anything
I know these winters are merely seasons of
bleakness that give way to dandelion fuzz and
spring showers
I know the sun will rise tomorrow morning and
the stars will twinkle their greetings at me
tomorrow night
I know impermanence is the beauty of moments
good, bad, and legendary
I know we all have a finite amount of breaths to
take and we should bask in them even when they
start to taste like shards of glass
I know summer will come back around and
she'll bring long walks and bonfires and sunsets
with the loves of my life
But I don't know anything

I know my laugh is one of my best friend's
favorite sounds
I know how it feels to drive 65 with all the
windows down and the music so loud it echoes
in my cells

I know what it feels like to jump headfirst into
the deep end not knowing how to swim
I know that funnel cake and chocolate ice cream
didn't always taste like failure
I know what it feels like to lose everything
But I don't know anything

I know the world would keep spinning on its
axis and daisies would bloom whether my heart
was still beating or not
But I don't KNOW anything

Dust

Maybe we are all stardust mixed with shadows
And maybe the shadows seem thicker than
sunlight
Maybe everything gets better
And maybe it doesn't

Maybe the future is beautiful
Maybe it's painful
Maybe everything gets worse
Maybe you leave today
And maybe you hold on

I hope that you hold on
For movie nights
For hugs from your friends
To tell one more stupid joke
To drink one more expensive coffee
To tell one more person in traffic to suck your
dick

Hold on
For the leaves changing colors again in the fall
Hold on
For the possibility of your colors changing too

Hold on because your pets will never understand
where their person went
Hold on
Because you still have air in your lungs right
now
And you aren't too far gone to come back
To resurface
To start again

Adventure

Your laugh was a strawberry starburst in my
head
Now it's just the wrapper
As empty as all of your pretty little lies

You wanted me for the adventure
Because I, cold and crazy and free, was
everything you knew she couldn't give you
But the thing you don't yet understand about
people
Is that they are not here to provide adventure
I was not put on this earth to "spice up" your life
I am not here to be the thing you only want
when you're bored

I don't care how much you say you want to kiss
me
To hold me
To lay in my bed and laugh with me
I don't care what you say anymore

I dont think you're a bad person
I think your path has led you somewhere you
weren't ready for

I think your mistakes led you to a choice you
weren't ready to make
A decision you didn't make
Because you love being comfortable
But I know you'll regret it
Somewhere down the line
When you hear my name
And you remember what we could have been
What could have happened if you broke her
heart
Instead of your own

But I will belong to the wind by then, darling
And you will still belong to her

M

I wish goodbyes were easier to say
I wish my mind didn't whisper your name in my
ear anymore
7 letters I just want to forget
7 letters that sound like a piano out of tune
A love song sang in the wrong key

I love you
I do
And I do believe that love is the strongest force
in the universe
I believe love gives life meaning
I believe if there's anything worth fighting for
In this ridiculous, painful little life
its love

But love is not always enough
Especially when its one sided
And I wish reality hadn't slammed into me like a
semi truck
Because I could've been happy being your
almost lover
For the rest of my life

But you would never ever admit
That you were mine

Birthday Cake

I want you to look at me and I want to trust the
reason for it
I want to believe you
But words are just pretty sounds until they start
to taste bitter
And I don't ever want to know what your eyes
look like when they go cold

Your laugh makes my head feel fuzzy
I want to snort lines of you
But I know the moment my caterpillars turn to
butterflies the game will change
Suddenly,
I am a moth
and you are the lamp I am catastrophically
pulled towards
All I can think about lately is what your smile
would taste like
What it could be like if it were your hand on my
cheek instead of my own

I wonder if we are more than a kaleidoscope of
missed connections in another universe
I wonder if we gave each other time, what might
happen

But we already know
Neither of us has the patience to wait for a cake
to rise

Sobriety

I can't reconcile the idea of sobriety with my
idea of myself
Who will I become when weeks stop being a
haze of moments that taste like rum and things I
can't remember
They say the grass is always greener but I fear
all of mine has been dead this whole time

The fuzz always starts in my fingertips and I
can't stop until I can feel it in my lungs
Everything glows when I've downed 19 shots
with no plans of stopping
I love the way the liquor sits in my emptiness
Fills me up enough that I start to look whole in
my reflection

Blood Ties

 I want to hate you but I don't know how
Your laugh still sounds like the first time I felt
safe
Your hug feels like my first sip of wine and the
slippery slope that followed
Every time my heart breaks I just want to call
you but we both know why I can't

I wonder what you'd say if you knew about the
drugs
I wonder how angry you'd be at me for growing
up and being different than you thought
I wish I could fucking talk to you
I wish you knew how to listen
I just want you to fucking understand
I hate the distance but when I'm with you I just
hate myself

I don't want to be the one to leave but you will
never understand why I can't stay
How do you expect my loyalty when you've
only ever given me emptiness

I don't understand you but I guess that means
we'll break even in the end

I hope you find your sunshine again

Not even you deserve to be sad forever

10-19-2022

These days I think of you with more indifference
than anger
And I wonder if I'll ever look at the memories
with a grain of fondness
Rather than the sting of regret
I don't regret the softness you dug out of me
And brought back to life
I don't regret the way that you reminded me
What it feels like for almost love to bloom in my
empty spaces
I don't regret the laughter we shared

I regret that I let you talk me into becoming
someone
I never wanted to be
I regret that you became my new obsession
With no regard for anything else
I regret being pulled so far into a complete
fucking fantasy
I am angry for what could never have been
No matter how much we wanted it
You talked us in so many circles
I thought being dizzy was the same thing as
being in love

I miss you sometimes
When my cats are running around
And I reach for my phone to send you a video
Forgetting, for a moment, that I said I never
want to speak to you again
I miss you when I let myself wonder if
In another life theres a version of us
That is more than misguided hope

Reality

My head is spinning and I can't tell if it's from
the alcohol
Your pleading
Or my own dishonesty
My own disrespect of myself

Your eyes don't look warm to me anymore
The strawberry milkshake you made in my head
Has gone sour

I used to say you felt like drugs to me
Soaring blissfully towards the sun
But every drug has its comedown
And this is by far my worst one

I thought taking bumps of you in shadowed
corners
Would satisfy the craving I couldn't explain
But every bump made me want more
Need more
More than you had ever planned on giving me

I didn't realize it then, but sparkly promises in
little bags
Aren't enough for me anymore

And when you told me to get clean
I didn't know you meant from you

Sobriety 2

I am afraid of sobriety because I never got the
chance to know my soul sans substance

Maybe all I am is a cloud of vapor
But I'd rather know that now
Before I am carried away on the wind

Maybe it's not too late to find out what my
favorite color is
Maybe my favorite meal isn't whatever bits of
powder I can lick out of a baggie

Maybe I am capable of hearing love songs and
thinking about a person instead of drugs

Maybe I am not a graveyard for hope and
possibility

I've been told relapse doesn't have to be
synonymous with farewell
And maybe it doesn't
If I am not ready to say goodbye

Addiction

Three days without you
And my skin feels like it's on fire
I've gone longer, sure
But never intentionally

I wonder sometimes who I would be
If we had never met
If you hadn't held my hand
Caressed my face
And made everything feel so warm
Through the worst moments of my life

I was smothered by you for half a decade
And never even realized i couldn't breathe
Never saw your hand around my throat for what
it was
But maybe it's not too late to remember
What the wind feels like

Silly Goose

I can't carry you around with me anymore
I don't know if this is goodbye or merely
repetition
Of thoughts and emotions with nowhere to go
now but out

I miss hiding grape tomatoes in your food
I miss the way seeing you made me feel better
I miss feeling like I was flying
I miss the things that almost happened
I miss you and I love you and I fucking hate you
all at once

I can't do this anymore

So much of me is lost
Pieces scattered in the wind like dandelion seeds
I wonder where they'll end up
Mount Fugi or a cemetery

I only feel real when my face is numb
And my stomach burns
From vodka or shame I can never tell
I don't know if there's a difference

Sometimes

Sometimes all I want to do is run
Faster than light
To disappear in seconds
My existence just a blip
End credits rolling across a screen
My name in the smallest print at the bottom

I wish I could erase the smile he wears when he
sees me
Because I know the sadness that would replace it
The agony
If I ever did decide to leave
Sometimes I wish he was capable of letting me
go
Sometimes I wish I wasn't the one still holding
on

11-30-2021

I am afraid that if you split me down the middle
To see the sum of my parts
There would be nothing left
No substance beyond what I can snort

I don't know who I am anymore
I want to hold on but I don't know how
I've never heard silence this loud

You tell me you love me
You hold me tighter than I've ever been held
But I am as good as dead

11-7-2022

I'm cutting lines with my library card
The lies drip from my mouth like honey
But my tongue is so numb I can't taste them
I can't see their affect
I don't know what I'm doing
I don't know why I'm letting this happen
I can't think straight anymore
All I know is
White. Sparkling.
Looks like snow

21

Abstinence feels like a fever dream in the face of
my affliction
I wonder if there is relief in death
Or merely silence that stretches on forever
I am not a good person
I don't know how to be

I don't want to be saved

I traded razor blades
For tequila and cocaine
And I don't know how to show you the
difference
Because I'm still cutting lines
They just don't bleed as much anymore

Ana

I wish I knew how to stop the calculator that
lives in my brain
I want buttered toast to taste like buttered toast
and not 232 calories and a walk around the block

I wish going to work wasn't washed in secrecy
and near fainting because my only meal of the
day happens at 2pm
490 calories in a spicy chicken sandwich
400 calories in an onion ring
So much shame in knowing they see my eating
disorder
But today I'm only working 12 hours

I have an eating disorder

I have an eating disorder

I have an eating disorder and its eating me alive

I'm hollowed out

How much time do I have left?